Let's Discover The States

South Central

ARKANSAS • KANSAS • LOUISIANA
MISSOURI • OKLAHOMA

By
Thomas G. Aylesworth
Virginia L. Aylesworth

CHELSEA HOUSE PUBLISHERS
New York   New Haven   Philadelphia

Created and produced by Blackbirch Graphics, Inc.

DESIGN: Richard S. Glassman
PROJECT EDITOR: Bruce S. Glassman
ASSOCIATE EDITOR: Robin Langley Sommer

First printing

Printed in Hong Kong

Manufactured by Oceanic Graphic Printing Productions

Library of Congress Cataloging-in-Publication Data
Aylesworth, Thomas G.
  South Central.

  (Let's discover the states)
  Includes bibliographies and index.
  Summary: Discusses the geographical, historical, and cultural aspects of Louisiana, Arkansas, Missouri, Kansas, and Oklahoma, using maps, illustrated fact spreads, and other illustrated material to highlight the land, history, and people of each individual state.
  1. Southwestern States—Juvenile literature. [1. Southern States. 2. Great Plains] I. Aylesworth, Virginia L. II. Title. III. Series: Aylesworth, Thomas G. Let's discover the states.
F396.A95 1988   976   87-18199
ISBN 1-55546-561-7

CONTENTS

The exuberance of the down-home music at the Ozark
   Folk Festival in Eureka Springs.
Sun shining on the deep blue waters of Lake Hamilton
   in the Ouachita Mountains.
The Buffalo River winding through forested hill
   country in the Ozarks.
The gleaming marble facade of the state capitol in
   Little Rock.
Eagles soaring in the sky over Holla Bend National
   Wildlife Refuge.
The majestic view of Blue Mountain Lake and the
   fertile fields of the Arkansas Valley from Magazine
   Mountain.

Let's Discover
Arkansas

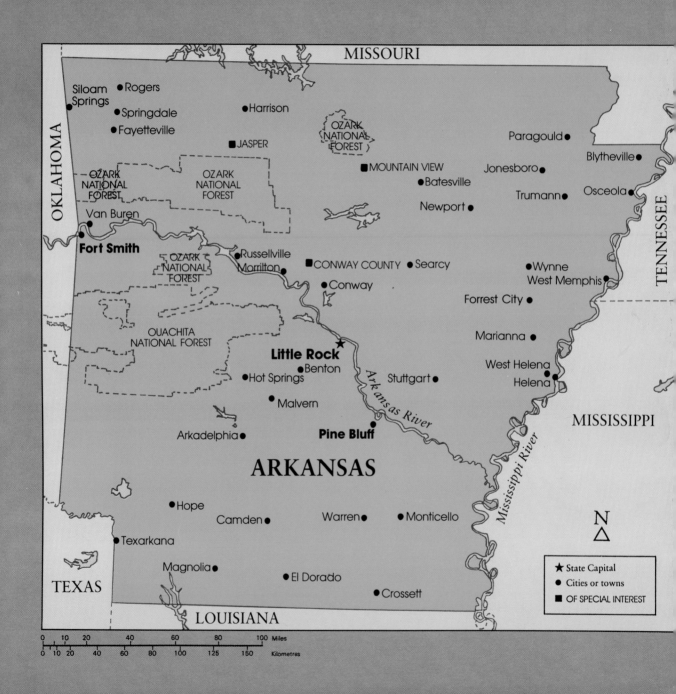

ARKANSAS
At a Glance

State Flag

Capital: Little Rock

Major Industries: Aluminum, fertilizer, forest products, livestock

Major Crops: Soybeans, rice, cotton, hay

State Flower:
Apple Blossom

State Bird:
Mockingbird

Size: 53,104 square miles (27th largest)

Population: 2,349,000 (33rd largest)

9

The Ozark Mountains, in northwestern Arkansas, have numerous springs, scenic plains, and rolling hills. Altitudes here can reach 2,000 feet.

The Land

Arkansas is bordered on the north by Missouri, on the east by Tennessee and Mississippi, on the south by Louisiana, and on the west by Oklahoma and Texas. There are five main land regions in the state: the Ozark Plateau, the Ouachita Mountains, the Arkansas Valley, the Mississippi Alluvial Plain, and the West Gulf Coastal Plain.

The Ozark Plateau, also called the Ozark Mountains, is part of a large land region that Arkansas shares with Illinois, Missouri, and Oklahoma. In Arkansas the Plateau is a wide strip extending from the northwest through the north central part of the state. It is a beautiful region with its rugged hills, deep valleys, and rushing streams, much of it covered by dense hardwood and pine forests. This part of the state supports beef and dairy cattle, poultry farms, hay fields, and fruit orchards.

Arkansas' famous Hot Springs are in the Ouachita Mountains. At this well-known health and recreation resort, the waters reach a natural temperature of 143 degrees Fahrenheit.

The Ouachita Mountains, in west-central Arkansas, extend into Oklahoma. This is a region of ridges and valleys, much of it unsuitable for farming. However, cattle, poultry, soybeans, and fruit can be raised where the land is not too steep. Timber is an important industry in the Ouachitas. Other resources here include sand, gravel, coal, and natural gas. This is also a region of hot springs and health resorts.

The Arkansas Valley lies between the Ozark Plateau and the Ouachita Mountains in the western two-thirds of the state. This hilly area includes the highest point in the state—Magazine Mountain, at 2,823 feet. The fertile fields here are ideal for raising vegetables, called truck crops, and there is good pasturage for beef cattle. Coal is mined in the Arkansas Valley, which also has extensive natural gas fields.

The Mississippi Alluvial Plain stretches along the eastern border of Arkansas and is part of the Mississippi River delta that runs from Missouri through Louisiana. This is low, level, fertile land, ideal for growing cotton, rice, soybeans, oats, and wheat.

The West Gulf Coastal Plain covers southeast and south central Arkansas and extends into Louisiana and Texas. Here are pine forests, natural gas and oil deposits, and fruit, vegetable, livestock, and poultry farms.

The most important rivers in Arkansas are the Mississippi, which forms the state's eastern boundary, the Arkansas, the Ouachita, the Red, the White, and the St. Francis. Arkansas has a few large natural lakes and numerous man-made lakes. Many springs of pure water are found in the mountainous areas, including the state's famous Mammoth Springs and Hot Springs.

Temperatures in Arkansas vary considerably from north to south, although the entire state has a warm, rainy climate. In July temperatures range from 78 degrees Fahrenheit in the northwest to 82 degrees F. in the southern areas; January temperatures range between 36 degrees F. and 48 degrees F. Rainfall averages 48 inches per year, and little snow falls except in the highlands, which may receive some 6 inches per year.

Crescent-shaped Lake Chicot, in southeastern Arkansas, is the state's largest natural body of water.

The History

There were Paleo-Indians in what would become Arkansas several thousand years before Europeans explored the area in the 16th and 17th centuries. The Caddo and the Quapaw, or Arkansa, were the principal tribes encountered by the explorers.

The Spanish were the first non-Indians to arrive, in 1541. Hernando de Soto and his party discovered the Mississippi River after marching overland from Florida, and they crossed the river near what is now Memphis, Tennessee. De Soto went on through the Arkansas region to the Ozark Mountains. More than a century later, in 1673, the French explorers Father Jacques Marquette and Louis Joliet traveled down the Mississippi River to the Arkansas River. In 1682, Robert Cavelier, known as La Salle, claimed the lands along the Mississippi for France, calling the territory Louisiana. This claim included what would become Arkansas. In 1686 Henri de Tonti, a friend of La Salle, set up a camp that grew into the first non-Indian settlement west of the Mississippi, Arkansas Post, at the mouth of the Arkansas River.

Fort Smith was built in 1817 to protect settlers against Indian attacks. Seventy years later, natural gas was discovered in the area, which brought new prosperity to the state.

Jacques Marquette was one of the first Europeans to visit what is now Arkansas. In 1673 Marquette journeyed into the region briefly and glimpsed its beauties with his fellow explorer Louis Joliet.

The French made a few unsuccessful attempts at settlement after that, but in 1763 Spain took over the land west of the Mississippi. In 1800 the Louisiana Territory was returned to France, which sold it to the United States in 1803. When the U.S. government divided up the Louisiana Territory, what is now Arkansas became part of the Missouri Territory. Fort Smith was built in 1817 to protect Arkansas settlers from Indian attacks, and settlements began to rise between the fort and Arkansas Post. The Arkansas Territory, which included part of present-day Oklahoma, was created in 1819. In 1836 Arkansas became the 25th state of the Union, with Little Rock as its capital.

Arkansas was divided on the question of slavery: before the Civil War broke out in 1861, the state voted to remain in the Union.

Augustus H. Garland was governor of Arkansas from 1874 to 1876 and served as U.S. Attorney General during the 1880s. Throughout his career, Garland was a dedicated leader in the cause of civil and political rights.

Pioneer teacher Albert Pike established one of the first schools in Arkansas. Later, he became one of the state's best-known and most influential lawyers.

However, when the United States asked for troops, Arkansas refused to send them and seceded from the Union to join the Confederacy. Even so, more than 10,000 Arkansas soldiers fought on the Union side during the war. Confederate troops in the state were forced into southern Arkansas after the Union victory at Pea Ridge in March 1862. Union troops captured Little Rock in 1863, and the Confederates set up a new capital at Washington, in southwestern Arkansas. The following year a Union state government was established at Little Rock by Arkansans opposed to the war, who drew up a new constitution that abolished slavery. These rival state governments continued until the war ended in 1865.

After the Civil War, federal troops occupied Arkansas from 1867 to 1874. During the late 1800s, the state's economy recovered from the years of conflict during and after the war and began to expand. Railroads were built, which brought new settlers into the state. Farming prospered, and the discovery of bauxite (aluminum ore) led to intensive mining. In the early 1900s, rice and soybean cultivation became important, as did the forest-products industry. Many former tenant farmers were able to buy land.

During World War II, farming and mining flourished to meet wartime demands, and new industries came into the state. By the 1950s the number of factories in Arkansas had doubled from the total operating before the United States entered the war in 1941. Arkansas was also an important area for training military personnel.

Today, Arkansas is still growing, economically and culturally. Petroleum, aluminum, processed foods, and forest products are integral parts of the state's economy. Tourism is increasingly important.

The year after Arkansas became a territory, its first school, Dwight Mission at Russellville, was established. The state legislature provided for a public-school system in 1843, the same year that the state's first library was founded in Little Rock. The first institution of higher education in Arkansas—Philander Smith College—was founded in 1868. By the turn of the century, there were six more colleges and universities in the state.

The Ozark Folk Center, in Mountain View, celebrates the cultural heritage of rural Arkansas with native crafts, folk and harvest festivals, and banjo, guitar, and fiddle contests.

The People

General Douglas MacArthur, a native of Little Rock, became one of the nation's foremost military leaders. He commanded Allied forces in the Pacific theater of operations during World War II.

Slightly more than half the people of Arkansas live in cities and towns, including Little Rock, Pine Bluff, Hot Springs, and Fort Smith. More than 99 percent of them were born in the United States. The largest single religious group in the state is Baptist, followed by the Episcopalians, Methodists, Presbyterians, Roman Catholics, and members of the Churches of Christ.

One of the best-known generals in American history, Douglas MacArthur, who served in three wars, was born near Little Rock. As Supreme Allied Commander of the Southwest Pacific Area in World War II, General MacArthur was a brilliant military strategist. His masterful use of land, sea, and air forces in the Philippines was a key factor in the eventual Japanese surrender on September 2, 1945. Architect Edward Durrell Stone, who designed museums and public buildings of international renown, was a native of Fayetteville. In the field of entertainment, Mary Steenburgen, the talented movie actress, was born in Newport, and Arkansas has produced two of the finest singers of country and western music—Glen Campbell (Billstown) and Johnny Cash (Kingsland).

Ozark Folk Center.

OF SPECIAL INTEREST

NEAR JASPER: *Diamond Cave*
This is one of the oldest caves in the United States, containing miles of strange and
    beautiful formations.
IN LITTLE ROCK: *MacArthur Park*
The park's Old Arsenal was the birthplace of General Douglas MacArthur, the
    Supreme Commander of Allied Forces in the Southwest Pacific during World
    War II.
NEAR MURFREESBORO: *Crater of Diamonds*
The nation's only diamond field, discovered by farmer John M. Huddleston in
    1906, has yielded gems worth up to $250,000.
IN HOT SPRINGS: *Hot Springs National Park*
This 4,700-acre park contains 47 springs from which flow some one million
    gallons of thermal water per day.
NEAR MOUNTAIN VIEW: *Ozark Folk Center*
This is a living museum of mountain heritage, crafts, and music. "Cabin crafts" are
    demonstrated and musicals are presented.

For more information write:
ARKANSAS DEPARTMENT OF PARKS AND TOURISM
1 CAPITOL MALL
LITTLE ROCK, ARKANSAS 72201

FURTHER READING

Ashmore, Harry S. *Arkansas: A Bicentennial History.* Norton, 1978.
Bradley, Donald M. *Arkansas: Its Land and People.* Little Rock Museum of
    Science and Industry, 1980.
Carpenter, Allan. *Arkansas*, rev. ed. Childrens Press, 1978.
Dougan, Michael B. *Confederate Arkansas: The People and Policies of a Frontier
    State in Wartime.* University of Alabama Press, 1976.
Fradin, Dennis B. *Arkansas in Words and Pictures.* Childrens Press, 1980.

The excitement of bidding for prize-winning cattle at
    the Mid-America Fair Auction in Topeka.
A walk through the past on Dodge City's notorious
    Front Street.
The colorful maypole dance at the Swedish Pioneers
    Festival in Lindsborg.
Mile after mile of golden wheat shining in the
    afternoon sun.
The simple grandeur of the Shawnee Mission outside
    Kansas City.
The stunning stained-glass windows of Bell Hall at
    Fort Leavenworth.

Let's Discover
Kansas

KANSAS
At a Glance

Capital: Topeka

Major Industries: Aircraft, petroleum products, farm machinery, agriculture

Major Crops: Wheat, sorghum, corn, hay

Size: 82,264 square miles (14th largest)
Population: 2,438,000 (32nd largest)

State Flag

State Bird:
Western Meadowlark

State Flower:
Sunflower

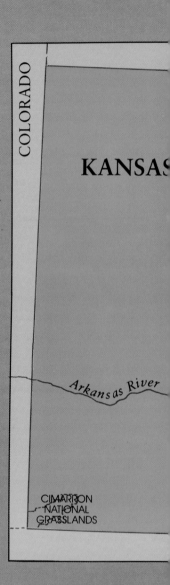

KANSAS

COLORADO

Arkansas River

CIMARRON
NATIONAL
GRASSLANDS

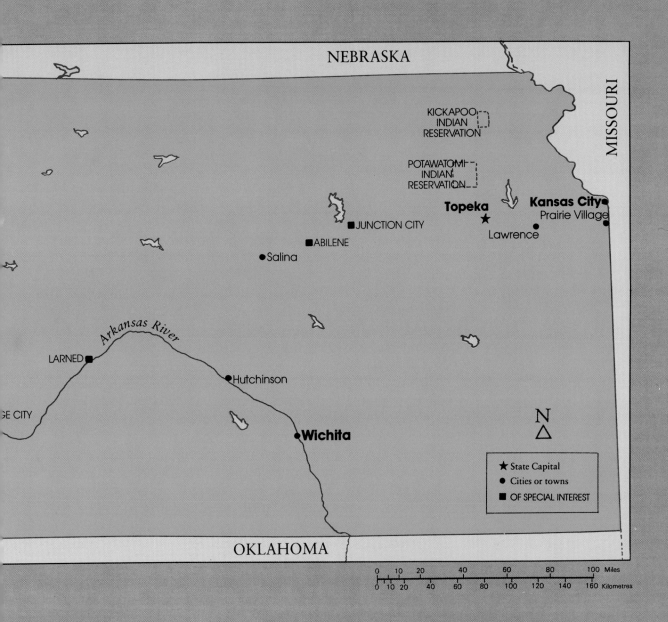

NEBRASKA

MISSOURI

KICKAPOO
INDIAN
RESERVATION

POTAWATOMI
INDIAN
RESERVATION

Topeka
★

Kansas City
Prairie Village

Lawrence

■JUNCTION CITY

■ABILENE

●Salina

Arkansas River

LARNED■

GE CITY

●Hutchinson

Wichita

N
△

★ State Capital
● Cities or towns
■ OF SPECIAL INTEREST

OKLAHOMA

| 0 | 10 | 20 | | 40 | | 60 | | 80 | | 100 | Miles |
| 0 | 10 | 20 | 40 | 60 | 80 | 100 | 120 | 140 | 160 | Kilometres |

The Land

Central Kansas combines high, hilly country and low-lying plains.

Much of western Kansas is vast, level prairie, ideal for grazing livestock. The state ranks among the nation's top four in total head of cattle.

Kansas is bounded on the west by Colorado, on the north by Nebraska, on the east by Missouri, and on the south by Oklahoma. There are three main land regions in the state: the Dissected Till Plains, the Southeastern Plains, and the Great Plains.

The Dissected Till Plains are in the northeastern corner of Kansas, which was covered by great glaciers during the Ice Age. These glaciers left deposits of rich soil, rocks, and other material called till. Later, rivers cut through (dissected) the soil and left high bluffs. It is a region of farms that grow corn, hay, and sorghum. Hogs, dairy and beef cattle, and poultry are raised here.

The Southeastern Plains extend down from the Dissected Till Plains to the Oklahoma border. Here are gently sloping grass-covered hills—good grazing land for beef and dairy cattle. Sorghum and soybeans are grown in the region, which also has coal mines and natural gas wells.

The Great Plains cover the western two-thirds of Kansas. The land is slightly rolling, and slopes up from east to west, from about 1,500 feet above sea level to 4,000 feet at the Colorado border. This is wheat country; sorghum and sugar beets are also grown. Beef cattle and sheep are raised here, and there are oil and natural gas wells.

Kansas has two main river systems: the Kansas, or Kaw, and the Arkansas. Most of Kansas's 150 lakes are man-made.

Blizzards, thunderstorms, tornadoes, and hailstorms are not uncommon in Kansas, due to the rapid changes in temperature that can occur as a result of air masses sweeping across the plains. Winters are cold, with temperatures averaging 32 degrees Fahrenheit. July temperatures range from the high 70s to the low 90s. Snowfall averages 17 inches per year, with total precipitation varying between 18 inches in the west and 40 inches in the southeast.

The History

Kansas was named for the Kansa, or Kaw, Indians who once lived on its eastern plains, which were also inhabited by the Osage, Pawnee, and Wichita tribes. These Indians were buffalo hunters and farmers, who raised beans, corn, and squash. On the western plains were non-farming buffalo hunters who followed the great herds of bison, including the Arapaho, Cheyenne, Comanche, Kiowa, and other tribes.

Kansas was part of the vast area claimed by France in the late 1600s, after French explorers had ventured into the region, followed by French fur trappers in the early 1700s. Like the Spanish, the French did not establish permanent settlements.

Most of present-day Kansas was included when the United States bought the Louisiana Territory from France in 1803, although Spain claimed a small southwestern section. Peaceful farming and hunting Indians were still the territory's principal inhabitants. In 1835 the federal government took land from numerous tribes in the East and relocated them onto Kansas land, divided into reservations. The tribes native to Kansas were also crowded onto reservations, as part of the government's policy of Indian removal and appropriation of Indian land. By 1842 some 30 tribes had moved into the territory, including the Chippewa, Delaware, Fox, Iowa, Kickapoo, Ottawa, Potawatomi, Sauk, Shawnee, and Huron, or Wyandot. American missionaries and settlers soon flocked in by the Santa Fe Trail.

The first permanent non-Indian settlement was Fort Leavenworth, established in 1827. As homesteaders demanded still more land, the government moved the Indians west again, this time to Oklahoma, a long-time hunting ground of the Plains Indians. Both hardship and bloodshed ensued, as the Indians saw their land and way of life disappearing.

Nine sandstone buildings comprise Fort Larned, established in 1859. Many Kansas military posts were built to protect travellers on the Santa Fe Trail from Indian attacks.

Temperance crusader Carry Nation attracted national attention in the late 1800s by wrecking Kansas saloons with her hatchet.

In the elections of 1855, the pro-slavery group won control of the territorial legislature in Kansas with the help of illegal votes from citizens of Missouri, a slave state, who crossed the border to sway the election. In 1856 pro-slavery men burned part of the town of Lawrence, a Free State stronghold. The violent abolitionist John Brown raided Potawatomie Creek, and five pro-slavery men were killed. Similar clashes resulted in more than 50 deaths, as the entire country waited for news from "Bleeding Kansas."

Finally, the Free Staters gained control of the legislature and repealed the pro-slavery laws. But because the state was now predominantly Republican, Democrats in Congress did not admit Kansas as the 34th state until 1861, after several southern states had already left the Union.

During the Civil War, Confederate raiders under William C. Quantrill burned most of Lawrence and killed about 150 citizens. Kansas sent many soldiers to the Union Army—in proportion to its population, more than any other state.

After the war, Kansas opened land to Union veterans and to freed slaves. Railroads brought new settlers and access to Eastern markets. Longhorn cattle were driven to Kansas depots from their Texas pastures. A hardy strain of winter wheat called Turkey Red was introduced by Mennonite immigrants from Russia, and wheat farming flourished. Kansas towns like Abilene, Wichita, and Dodge City became symbols of the wild frontier. For 10 years after 1875, Dodge City was the largest cattle market in the world.

In the early 20th century, coal, zinc, and lead mining and drilling for oil and natural gas brought new income and industry to Kansas, but wheat farming remained the state's principal business. During the Great Depression of the 1930s, farm output declined, prices dropped, and many farmers had to declare bankruptcy. Banks failed and factories closed. A long drought caused a large area of the Kansas plains to become part of what was known as the Dust Bowl. But World War II brought demand for farm and mineral products from Kansas. War planes were produced in Wichita, and many military bases were built in the state.

The People

Almost 67 percent of the people in Kansas live in cities and towns, including Kansas City, Topeka, and Wichita. The largest religious groups are the Methodists and Roman Catholics, followed by the Baptists, Episcopalians, Lutherans, Presbyterians, and other Christian denominations.

Famous Kansans include the distinguished educator Milton Eisenhower, who was born in Abilene. The brother of general and president Dwight D. Eisenhower, he served as president of three American universities. President Eisenhower, although he was born in Texas, spent his boyhood in Abilene. Psychiatrists Karl and William Menninger, co-founders with their father of the renowned Menninger Clinic and Foundation for the treatment of mental disorders, were born in Topeka. The legendary jazz saxophonist Charlie "Bird" Parker was a native of Kansas City, and playwright William Inge, the Pulitzer Prize-winning author of *Picnic*, *Bus Stop*, and *Come Back, Little Sheba*, was born in Independence.

Far left:
Aviator Amelia Earhart was a native of Atchison. She was the first woman to fly the Atlantic as a passenger and made aviation history as a pilot on long-distance solo flights.

Above:
Dwight D. Eisenhower, the 34th president of the United States, spent most of his childhood in Abilene, a major railroad center during the "cattle kingdom" days of the mid- to late 1800s.

25

The Kansas Cosmosphere & Discovery Center, in Hutchinson, is one of the state's most popular attractions.

OF SPECIAL INTEREST

IN ABILENE: *Eisenhower Library and Museum*
The mementos and papers of President Dwight D. Eisenhower, who grew up in Abilene, are housed here. His boyhood home is nearby.

NEAR LARNED: *Fort Larned National Historic Site*
Many of the buildings of this frontier fort have been restored. It was built to protect travelers on the Santa Fe Trail.

IN DODGE CITY: *Front Street*
This is the colorful main street of old-time Dodge City, which has been restored to look as it did in the days of "Bat" Masterson and "Wild Bill" Hickok.

NEAR JUNCTION CITY: *Fort Riley*
On the grounds of this old U.S. Army cavalry center stand an early Kansas capitol building (the state had four capitals before Topeka) and General George A. Custer's home.

IN WICHITA: *Old Cowtown Museum*
This is a 40-building village depicting Wichita life from 1865 to 1880.

For more information write:
THE TRAVEL AND TOURISM DIVISION
DEPARTMENT OF ECONOMIC DEVELOPMENT
503 KANSAS AVENUE, 6TH FLOOR
TOPEKA, KANSAS 66603

FURTHER READING

Carpenter, Allan. *Kansas*, rev. ed. Childrens Press, 1981.
Davis, Kenneth S. *Kansas: A Bicentennial History*. Norton, 1976.
Fradin, Dennis B. *Kansas in Words and Pictures*. Childrens Press, 1981.
Ikenberry, Larry D. *Kansas Past: A Photographic Essay of the Great Plains of Western Kansas*. Cascade Photographics, 1979.
Kansas: A Guide to the Sunflower State. Somerset, 1939.
Richmond, Robert W. *Kansas: A Land of Contrasts*, 2nd ed. Forum Press, 1980.

The soaring 450-foot State Capitol surrounded by 27 acres of parklike grounds in Baton Rouge.

The sights, sounds, smells, and tastes of the French Market in New Orleans.

Authentic jazz, revelry, floats, and costumes enlivening the Mardi Gras celebration.

Silence and serenity around the monument to Evangeline in St. Martinville.

The hauntingly beautiful cypress swamps near Lake Charles.

Peaceful verdant trails in Fontainbleau Park in St. Tammany Parish.

Let's Discover
Louisiana

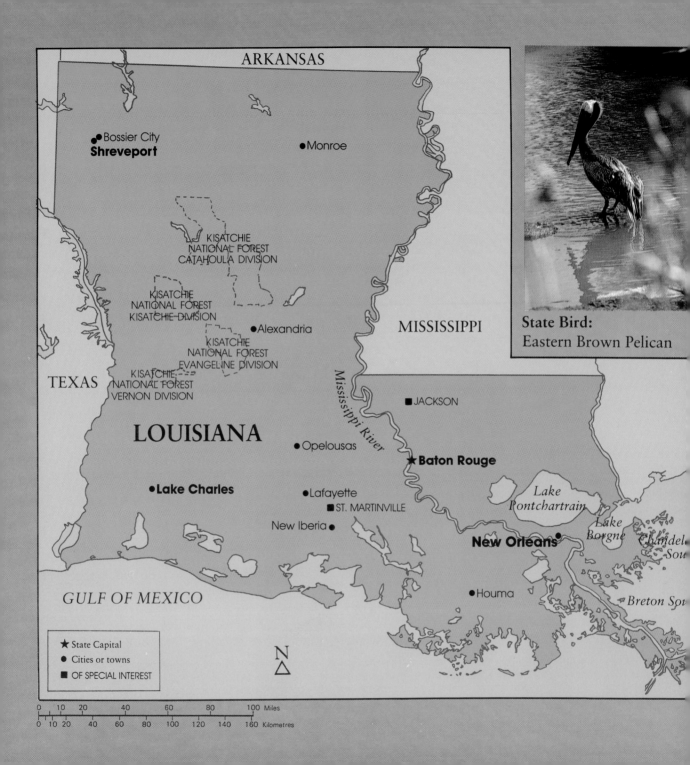

ARKANSAS

●Bossier City
Shreveport

●Monroe

KISATCHIE
NATIONAL FOREST
CATAHOULA DIVISION

KISATCHIE
NATIONAL FOREST
KISATCHIE DIVISION

●Alexandria

KISATCHIE
NATIONAL FOREST
EVANGELINE DIVISION

TEXAS

KISATCHIE
NATIONAL FOREST
VERNON DIVISION

LOUISIANA

MISSISSIPPI

Mississippi River

■ JACKSON

●Opelousas

★**Baton Rouge**

●**Lake Charles**

●**Lafayette**
■ ST. MARTINVILLE

*Lake
Pontchartrain*

New Iberia ●

New Orleans●

*Lake
Borgne*

*Chandel
Sou*

GULF OF MEXICO

●Houma

Breton Sou

★ State Capital
● Cities or towns
■ OF SPECIAL INTEREST

N
△

| 0 | 10 | 20 | | 40 | | 60 | | 80 | | 100 | Miles |
| 0 | 10 | 20 | 40 | 60 | 80 | 100 | 120 | 140 | 160 | Kilometres |

State Bird:
Eastern Brown Pelican

LOUISIANA

At a Glance

State Flower: Magnolia

State Flag

Capital: Baton Rouge

Major Industries: Chemical products, transportation equipment, electronics, petroleum

Major Crops: Soybeans, sugarcane, rice, cotton

Size: 48,523 square miles (31st largest)

Population: 4,462,000 (18th largest)

31

Louisiana's marshy coastal region, in the southern part of the state, is dotted with lagoons and lakes.

Slow-moving bodies of water called *bayous* help drain Louisiana's many swamps.

The Land

Louisiana is bordered on the west by Texas, on the north by Arkansas, on the east by Mississippi, and on the south by the Gulf of Mexico. The state has three main land regions: the East Gulf Coastal Plain, the Mississippi Alluvial Plain, and the West Gulf Coastal Plain.

The East Gulf Coastal Plain is located east of the Mississippi River and north of Lake Pontchartrain. Its southern section has extensive marshland, rising to low hills in the north.

The Mississippi Alluvial Plain is located along the lower Mississippi River, extending north and south from the Arkansas line to the Gulf of Mexico. The region contains broad, low ridges and hollows and, to the south, the great Mississippi Delta—formed by silt carried down to the mouth of the river. Here is some of the most fertile soil in Louisiana.

The West Gulf Coastal Plain comprises the western half of the state. In the south it is a region of marshes. Farther north are the Louisiana prairies, succeeded by higher land extending toward Arkansas. A variety of farms in western Louisiana produce grain crops, peanuts, and beef and dairy cattle. Industry benefits from oil and natural gas wells and extensive stands of timber.

Louisiana's coastline measures some 397 miles in length. But if the bays, offshore islands, and river mouths are included, the coastline is 7,721 miles long. Only Alaska and Florida have longer tidal shorelines. The most important rivers in the state are the Mississippi, the Atchafalaya, and the Red. The largest lake in the state is Lake Pontchartrain, once an arm of the sea, which is filled with salt water. Numerous bayous in the Mississippi Delta drain excess water from the region's lakes and rivers. Louisiana, with 53 inches of rainfall annually, is one of the wettest states in the country. Hot and humid in the summer, southern Louisiana has temperatures of more than 80 degrees Fahrenheit. Winter temperatures rarely fall below 50 to 55 degrees F.

The History

When the first European explorers arrived, some 12,000 Indians were living in what was to become Louisiana. They belonged to several dozen tribes, among them the Atakapa, the Caddo, the Chitimacha, and the Tunica. Most of them lived on the banks of rivers and bayous, where they built huts of poles and palmetto leaves, sometimes plastered with mud. To provide food, the women farmed, and the men hunted and fished.

The Spanish explorer Hernando de Soto was the first European to see the Louisiana area, when he arrived in 1541 on a fruitless search for gold. He died there the next year, and the Spanish made no attempt to explore the territory further. The French explorer Robert Cavelier, called La Salle, arrived in 1682 with his band of 50 men. They had come down the Mississippi from the Great Lakes region. La Salle claimed the vast Mississippi Valley for France, naming it Louisiana for King Louis XIV.

Pierre Le Moyne, known as d'Iberville, came to the region in 1699, founding a French settlement at what is now Ocean Springs, Mississippi. The first permanent non-Indian settlement in present-day Louisiana was made by French colonists on the Red River at Natchitoches in 1714. In 1718 the governor of Louisiana, d'Iberville's brother, Jean Baptiste Le Moyne, began to construct New Orleans at the mouth of the Mississippi River. The new city became the capital of the colony in 1722.

France was disappointed in the financial return on its investment in the colony, and in 1762 it ceded to Spain the Isle of Orleans, which included New Orleans, and Louisiana land west of the Mississippi River. Under Spanish rule, Louisiana prospered and developed an important sugar industry. But in 1800 France renewed its interest in the region and negotiated with Spain to return the territory, which it did in 1803. France then promptly sold the entire Louisiana Territory to the United States for about $15 million. French and Spanish

Beginning in 1701, French Louisiana was governed by Jean Baptiste Le Moyne, who founded New Orleans in 1718. He named it in honor of the Duc d'Orleans, regent of France.

The Battle of New Orleans, on January 8, 1815, was a resounding victory over the British for American general Andrew Jackson and his forces in the last action of the War of 1812.

Huey Long, governor of Louisiana from 1928 to 1932 and U.S. senator from 1932 to 1935, was one of the state's most powerful political figures. Long, born in Winnifield, established a "political machine" that gave him almost total control of state government.

settlers were surprised to learn that their homeland was becoming part of the United States. By this time some 4,000 French residents o Acadia, eastern Canada—the Cajuns, as they were called—had moved into Louisiana.

In 1804 Congress divided up the Louisiana Territory, and one par became the Territory of Orleans, which was about the same area as the present state of Louisiana. In 1812 the territory was admitted to the Union as the 18th state. During the War of 1812, the British tried to capture the port of New Orleans in a battle that began in December 1814. On January 8, 1815, the British were defeated by General Andrew Jackson and his 4500-man force of frontiersmen. Neither side was aware that the victory occurred two weeks after a peace treaty had been signed by the United States and Great Britain.

The Civil War, in which Louisiana left the Union to join the Confederacy in 1861, ruined the state's economy, which had prospered as a result of heavy steamboat traffic on the Mississippi beginning in 1812. Union forces occupied New Orleans in 1862 and eventually controlled the entire state. There was widespread destruction of property. Not until the late 19th century did the economy begin to recover, as railroads expanded, roads and waterways were improved, and commerce resumed. Oil was discovered in 1901, and natural gas in 1916.

During World War II, many new industries began, including shipbuilding. The chemical and oil industries boomed. In the years between 1940 and 1960, the number of factories and plants increased about 60 percent. Today, Louisiana is still prospering as a center of national and international commerce. The addition of new products, as in the aerospace industry, has contributed to its growth.

The first school in what is now Louisiana was founded in New Orleans in 1725 by Roman Catholic monks. In 1727 Ursuline nuns started a girls' school that is still operating. The first public school was established by the Spanish in 1772, and in 1845 the state-wide public school system began. Lousiana's first library opened in New Orleans in 1804, and the New Orleans Public Library, established in 1843, was the state's first free library.

Perhaps the best-known feature of Louisiana's social life is the week-long succession of parades and festivals called Mardi Gras. Held each year before Lent, the New Orleans carnival attracts thousands of visitors to the city.

The People

Almost 69 percent of the people in Louisiana live in towns and cities, such as New Orleans and Baton Rouge. The state is unusual in that culturally it can almost be considered two states: a French, Roman Catholic south, and an Anglo-Saxon, Protestant north. Many people in the south are descendants of the original French and Spanish settlers; they call themselves Creoles. Another southern group is descended from the French settlers who were driven from the Acadian section of Canada by the British in 1755—the Cajuns. Many Louisiana southerners speak both French and English. In the north, most of the people are descendants of pioneers who came to the area from surrounding states. About a third of the people in Louisiana are Roman Catholics. Other large religious groups are the Baptists, Episcopalians, Methodists, and Presbyterians.

Louisiana has a strong literary heritage: novelist Truman Capote (best remembered for *In Cold Blood*) and Lillian Hellman (the author of such plays as *The Little Foxes*) were both born in New Orleans. The state has produced its fair share of musicians, too. The fine classical pianist Van Cliburn was born in Shreveport. Jazz trumpeters Louis Armstrong and Al Hirt were natives of New Orleans. Rock 'n' roll stars include Fats Domino (New Orleans) and Jerry Lee Lewis (Ferriday). In sports, Louisiana has produced one of the nation's greatest basketball players: Bill Russell, who was born in Monroe.

Playwright Lillian Hellman, born in New Orleans, wrote such powerful dramas as *The Little Foxes* (1939) and *Watch on the Rhine* (1941).

Hodges Gardens, south of Many, Louisiana, contains acres of flowering plants and wild animals.

OF SPECIAL INTEREST

IN NEW ORLEANS: *The Vieux Carré*
The French Quarter, with its old buildings adorned with wrought-iron balconies, St. Louis Cathedral, the French Market, and other historic sights, is also the home of great food and fine jazz. Mardi Gras takes over the whole city every year before Lent begins.

IN ST. MARTINVILLE: *St. Martin of Tours Catholic Church*
This church was built in 1838 as the mother church of the exiled Acadians, and it contains many beautiful artifacts.

IN JACKSON: *Milbank*
This columned Greek Revival townhouse was constructed in 1836, at a time when Louisiana planters and merchants built many impressive estates.

IN BATON ROUGE: *Old State Capitol*
Built in 1847 and burned during the Civil War, this historic building was restored in 1880 and used until the 1930s.

For more information write:
DEPARTMENT OF CULTURE, RECREATION AND TOURISM
POST OFFICE BOX 44291
CAPITOL STATION
BATON ROUGE, LOUISIANA 70804

FURTHER READING

Carpenter, Allan. *Louisiana*, rev. ed. Childrens Press, 1978.
Davis, Edwin A. *Louisiana: The Pelican State*, 4th ed. Louisiana State University Press, 1975.
Fradin, Dennis B. *Louisiana in Words and Pictures*. Childrens Press, 1981.
Huber, Leonard V. *Louisiana: A Pictorial History*. Scribners, 1975.
Kniffen, Fred B. *Louisiana: Its Land and People*. Louisiana State University Press, 1968.
Louisiana: A Guide to the State. Hastings, 1971

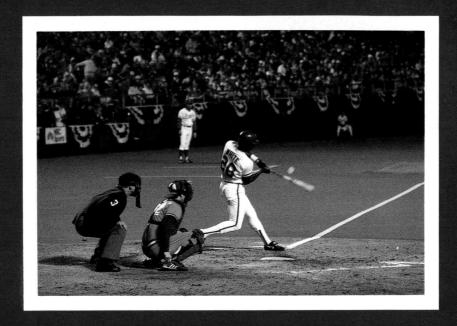

The beauty and simplicity of Mark Twain's boyhood
   home in Hannibal.
The sun sparkling off the clear waters of the giant Lake
   of the Ozarks.
An old-time sternwheeler churning the waters of the
   mighty Mississippi River.
Cows grazing in the rich pastures of the Mississippi
   Alluvial Plain.
The soaring 630-foot arch at the Jefferson National
   Expansion Memorial in St. Louis.
Cheering baseball fans at the beautiful Royals Stadium
   in Kansas City.

Let's Discover
Missouri

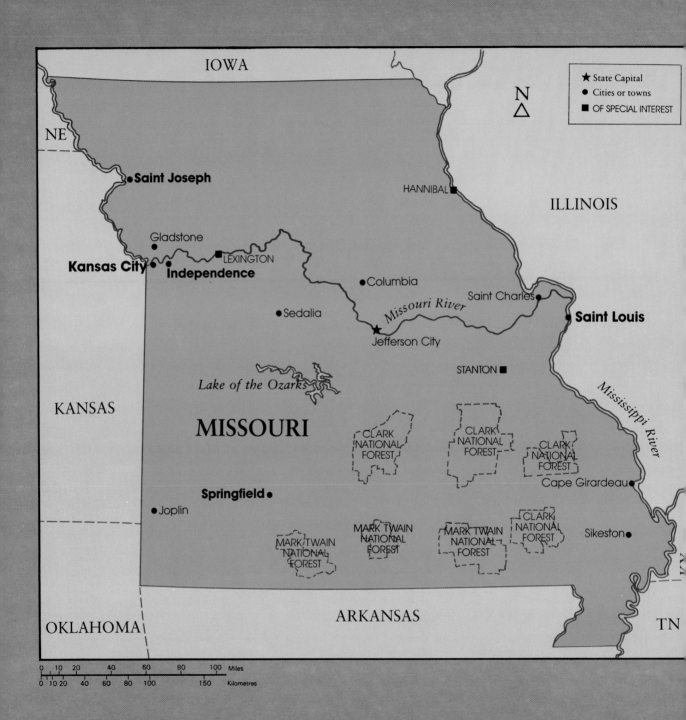

IOWA

NE

★ State Capital
● Cities or towns
■ OF SPECIAL INTEREST

N
△

● Saint Joseph

HANNIBAL ■

ILLINOIS

Gladstone ●

■ LEXINGTON

Kansas City ●
● Independence

● Columbia

Saint Charles
● Saint Louis

● Sedalia

Missouri River

KANSAS

★
Jefferson City

STANTON ■

Lake of the Ozarks

MISSOURI

Mississippi River

CLARK
NATIONAL
FOREST

CLARK
NATIONAL
FOREST

CLARK
NATIONAL
FOREST

Cape Girardeau ●

Springfield ●

● Joplin

MARK TWAIN
NATIONAL
FOREST

MARK TWAIN
NATIONAL
FOREST

MARK TWAIN
NATIONAL
FOREST

CLARK
NATIONAL
FOREST

Sikeston ●

OKLAHOMA

ARKANSAS

TN

0 10 20   40   60   80   100 Miles
0 10 20   40   60   80   100   150 Kilometres

MISSOURI
At a Glance

State Flag

State Flower: Hawthorn

Capital: Jefferson City

Major Industries: Transportation equipment, electronics, chemicals, agriculture

Major Crops: Soybeans, corn, wheat, cotton

Size: 69,686 square miles (19th largest)

Population: 5,008,000 (15th largest)

State Bird: Bluebird

41

The Lake of the Ozarks, in west-central Missouri, is the state's largest man-made lake. This region draws many vacationers to its attractive resorts.

Southeastern Missouri is part of the Mississippi Alluvial Plain and has the rich soil of a great river delta.

The Land

Missouri is bounded on the west by Oklahoma, Kansas, and Nebraska; on the north by Iowa; on the east by Illinois, Kentucky, and Tennessee; and on the south by Arkansas. The state has four main land regions: the Dissected Till Plains, the Osage Plains, the Ozark Plateau, and the Mississippi Alluvial Plain.

The Dissected Till Plains are located in the north, just above the Missouri River. During the Ice Age, these lands were covered by glaciers that left a deep deposit of fertile soil, well watered by numerous streams.

The Osage Plains form a triangular section in the west central part of Missouri. The land here is flat, with an occasional low hill.

The Ozark Plateau is a large area extending south from the Dissected Till Plains and the Osage Plains. This is higher country, with forested hills and small mountains. It is a scenic region, with many caves, large springs, and lakes. In addition to dairy and poultry farms, there are corn, oat, sorghum, fruit, and wheat farms. Some of the region's natural resources are coal, clay, zinc, lead, marble, granite, iron ore, and limestone.

The Mississippi Alluvial Plain covers the southeastern tip of the state. The area was once a swamp, but it has been drained and the silt-rich soil is unusually fertile. This "Boot Heel," as the southern plain is called, produces cotton, corn, soybeans, and fruit.

The most important rivers in the state are the Mississippi and the Missouri, which are the nation's longest rivers. The largest lake in the state is the man-made Lake of the Ozarks, a popular recreation center of 60,000 acres with a shoreline of more than 1,300 miles.

Missouri's size and position account for a wide range of climate and temperature, with the average annual temperature at 50 degrees Fahrenheit in the northwest, 60 degrees F. in the southeast. Rainfall and other forms of precipitation average from 48 inches per year in the southeast to 32 inches in the northwest.

The History

When the first European explorers arrived in the 17th century, a number of Indian tribes occupied the region's hills and plains. In east-central Missouri there were the Missouri Indians. To the south and west were the Osage, and in the north were the Fox, the Sauk, and others.

Like many parts of the Midwest, Missouri was first explored by the French. In 1673 Father Jacques Marquette and Louis Joliet descended the Mississippi and became the first non-Indians to see the mouth of the Missouri River. Another French explorer, Robert Cavelier, known as La Salle, voyaged down the Mississippi in 1682 and claimed the Mississippi Valley for France. He named the region Louisiana, for King Louis XIV.

French trappers and fur traders began establishing trading posts along the Mississippi, and French missionaries came to spread Christianity among the Indians. About 1700 some of these missionaries founded the first non-Indian settlement in Missouri—the Mission of St. Francis Xavier, near present-day St. Louis, which was soon abandoned because of the unhealthful swamps nearby. A permanent settlement was established in 1735, at Ste. Genevieve on the Mississippi River, where lead had been discovered some years before. In 1764 St. Louis, several miles to the north, was founded by Pierre Laclède Liguest and René Auguste Chouteau. St. Louis was originally a base for fur-trading operations, which were the state's most important industry for decades to come.

France gave up its territory west of the Mississippi to Spain in 1762, and the Spanish government encouraged American settlers to come into the region. One of these pioneers from the East was Daniel Boone, the legendary frontiersman. The Spanish granted him some 800 acres of land in what is now St. Charles County and eventually appointed him a judge.

President Thomas Jefferson bought the vast Louisiana Territory from Napoleon Bonaparte, emperor of France, in 1803. Much of this land was unexplored, and Jefferson called on the surveying skills of Meriwether Lewis and William Clark. Their expedition left St. Louis in 1804 and mapped the Northwest in to the Pacific Ocean before returning 1806.

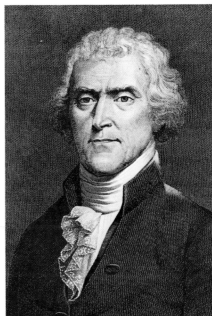

A view of St. Louis during the 1840s, when the city prospered by selling supplies to pioneers who planned to forge West.

St. Louis, the largest city in Missouri, has a population of more than 450,000. The city's famous 630-foot arch was designed by Eero Saarinen as a monument to westward expansion.

By 1800 Napoleon Bonaparte had become the ruler of France, and had forced Spain to return the lands west of the Mississippi. Napoleon then sold this vast region—an area three times greater tha that of the original 13 colonies—to the United States in the Louisian Purchase of 1803. When Missouri became part of the United States that year, its settlements became the staging ground for western expansion all the way to the Pacific Ocean. The expedition of Meriwether Lewis and William Clark began and ended in Missouri in 1804–1806.

The Missouri Territory was organized in 1812. In 1818 Missouri requested admission to the Union, but Congress delayed action during a national debate that lasted for several years, because many Missourians were slave owners. At the time, there were exactly as many slave states as free states, and the admission of Missouri as a slave state would upset the balance in the Senate. The result was the Missouri Compromise of 1820, in which Maine was to be admitted as a free state and Missouri as a slave state, with the proviso that slavery would not be permitted in any other state formed from the Louisiana Purchase north of Missouri's southern boundary. Missour entered the Union in 1821 as the 24th state.

Both the Santa Fe and Oregon Trails originated in Independence, and from the 1840s St. Louis grew wealthy outfitting wagon trains for the trek west. Later, great cattle herds would be driven into Missouri from the Southwest, destined for the stockyards of Kansas City.

In 1857 fresh controversy on the slavery issue broke out when the U.S. Supreme Court issued the Dred Scott Decision. It decreed that Scott, a Missouri slave, had no rights of citizenship because he was merely property, and that state laws banning slavery were unconstitutional in depriving persons of their property without due process of law.

On the eve of the Civil War in 1861, Missouri delegates voted to remain in the Union, but when hostilities broke out, Governor Claiborne F. Jackson refused to send troops. The state militia clashed

with Union soldiers at Boonville in July 1861, and federal forces took ontrol of northern Missouri. Governor Jackson and his troops eorganized and fought the Union soldiers again, this time at Wilson's Creek. The militia won the bloody battle, but Missouri was till torn by internal dissension about whether it should formally ecede from the Union. In October 1861, the legislature voted to join he Confederacy, but there were not enough members present to give his decision the force of law. Confederate General Sterling Price ried to gain control of Missouri, but was defeated at Westport, a part of present-day Kansas City, in 1864. Throughout the Civil War, bands of Union and Confederate raiders clashed in the state, destroying life and property.

St. Louis and Kansas City became increasingly important ransportation centers after the war ended in 1865, and the economy of the state flourished. In 1904 St. Louis celebrated its prosperity by hosting a World's Fair—the Lousiana Purchase Centennial Exposition. Some 20 million visitors attended.

The resources of Missouri were important to the armed forces during World War I. Coal and lead mining, manufacturing, and agriculture expanded. But the Great Depression of the 1930s interrupted this growth, as many mines and factories closed down and agricultural prices dropped. Federal and state programs were set up to provide relief and recovery. World War II accelerated the development of new industries between 1941 and 1945. Food processing, uranium and iron mining, chemicals, and electronics have diversified Missouri's economy, while agriculture remains important to the state.

The first school in Missouri, an elementary school in St. Louis, was established in 1774. The state system of public education was created in 1839. By the time Missouri was admitted to the Union, in 1821, there were two institutions of higher education in the territory—Cardinal Glennon College and Saint Louis University—both founded in 1818. Only 40 years after statehood, there were nine more colleges and universities in the state.

The Pony Express was a network of relay stations by which rugged young men carried the mail on horseback through the dangerous territories of the sparsely settled West. Missouri's position as the "gateway to the West resulted in the selection of St. Joseph as the starting point for Pony Express riders who raced to Sacramento, California, during 1860. The service was replaced by a transcontinental telegraph system in 1861.

45

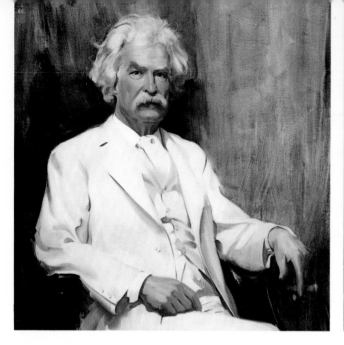

The People

Above:
Mark Twain, born Samuel Clemens in Florida in 1835, grew up in Hannibal to become one of America's most prominent and colorful writers. His life on and near the Mississippi River is reflected in such classics as *The Adventures of Huckleberry Finn.*

Above right:
Harry S. Truman, the 33rd president of the United States, was born in Lamar. As vice-president, he succeeded Franklin D. Roosevelt, who died in office during World War II. Truman authorized the use of atomic bombs against Hiroshima and Nagasaki, Japan, to force the Japanese surrender of September 2, 1945.

About 68 percent of the people in Missouri live in cities and towns, including St. Louis, Kansas City, Springfield, and St. Joseph. More than 98 percent of the residents of the state were born in the United States. Most of them had Czech, English, French, German, Irish, Italian, Polish, or Swiss ancestors. More than half of Missourians are Protestant, primarily Baptists, Disciples of Christ, Episcopalians, Lutherans, Methodists, Presbyterians, and members of the United Church of Christ About one in six Missourians is Roman Catholic.

American history has been enriched by many men and women from Missouri. Harry S. Truman, the 33rd president of the United States, was born in Lamar. The commander of the American Expeditionary Force in World War I, General John J. "Black Jack" Pershing, was a native of Laclede. A commander in the Allied invasion of Normandy, which resulted in an end to Nazi power in Europe during World War II, General Omar N. Bradley, came from Clark.

Missouri has also been prominent in the field of the arts. The painter Thomas Hart Benton was born in Neosho. Novelist Mark Twain, the author of *Huckleberry Finn* and *The Adventures of Tom Sawyer*, was born Samuel Clemens in Florida. Other distinguished writers from Missouri include the author of *Little Boy Blue*, Eugene Field (St. Louis), and the poets Langston Hughes (Joplin) and T. S. Eliot (St. Louis).

George Washington Carver, the scientist best known for his work with soybeans, was born in Diamond Grove. Two Missourians famous in Wild West days were the train robber Jesse James (born near Centerville, which is now Kearney) and "Calamity Jane" Cannary, the tomboy of the West (Princeton).

Missourians prominent in the field of classical music include operatic star Grace Bumbry (St. Louis) and opera conductress Sarah Caldwell (Maryville). Actors and actresses include Ed Asner (Kansas City), Linda Blair, Kevin Kline, and Vincent Price (St. Louis), Ginger Rogers (Independence), and Dick Van Dyke (West Plains).

Far left:
Agricultural scientist and teacher George Washington Carver was a native of Diamond Grove. He is best remembered for his pioneering work in developing products made from peanuts and sweet potatoes.

At left:
Writer Langston Hughes was born in Joplin. His work, including the play *Mulatto* (1935), focused attention on racial problems in the United States.

The Mark Twain Home and Museum.

OF SPECIAL INTEREST

IN INDEPENDENCE: *Harry S. Truman Library and Museum*
This modern building houses a reproduction of the 33rd president's White House office and many other exhibits and memorabilia.

NEAR STANTON: *Meramec Cave*
This huge cave is the legendary hideout of the outlaw Jesse James.

IN HANNIBAL: *Mark Twain Home and Museum*
The restored boyhood home of this great American writer contains many mementoes of his life and travels. Nearby is the Mark Twain Cave, which figures in *The Adventures of Tom Sawyer*.

IN THE OZARK PLATEAU: *Lake of the Ozarks*
This 60,000-acre lake is a popular recreation center that winds through the heart of the scenic Ozarks.

IN ST. LOUIS: *Jefferson National Expansion Memorial*
This huge complex, including the nation's tallest arch, commemorates St. Louis's historic role as the Gateway to the West.

For more information write:
MISSOURI DIVISION OF TOURISM
BOX 1055
JEFFERSON CITY, MISSOURI 65102

FURTHER READING

Bailey, Bernadine. *Picture Book of Missouri*, rev. ed. Whitman, 1974.
Carpenter, Allan. *Missouri*, rev. ed. Childrens Press, 1978.
Fradin, Dennis B. *Missouri in Words and Pictures*. Childrens Press. 1980.
Lyle, Wes. *Missouri: Faces and Places*. Regents Press of Kansas, 1977.
Nagel, Paul C. *Missouri: A Bicentennial History*. Norton, 1977.
Parrish, William E., and others. *Missouri: The Heart of the Nation*. Forum Press, 1980.

The roar of combines harvesting acres of rippling
    wheat.
Sparkling Honey Creek cascading into a pool at Turner
    Falls.
Colorfully garbed Indians performing native dances
    near Anadarko.
Prime cattle being judged at the Washita County Fair
    in Cordell.
Skyscrapers and oil pumps rising from the prairie at
    Oklahoma City.
A panoramic view of the Wichita Mountains and the
    nearby fertile plains.

Let's Discover
Oklahoma

OKLAHOMA
At a Glance

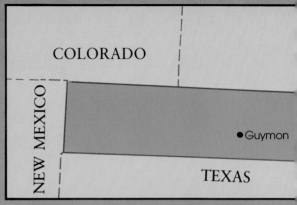

COLORADO

NEW MEXICO

TEXAS

● Guymon

Capital: Oklahoma City

Major Industries: Oil-field machinery, petroleum, agriculture

Major Crops: Wheat, cotton, sorghum, peanuts, hay, soybeans

State Flag

Size: 69,919 square miles (18th largest)

Population: 3,298,000 (25th largest)

State Flower: Mistleto

State Bird: Scissortailed Flycatcher

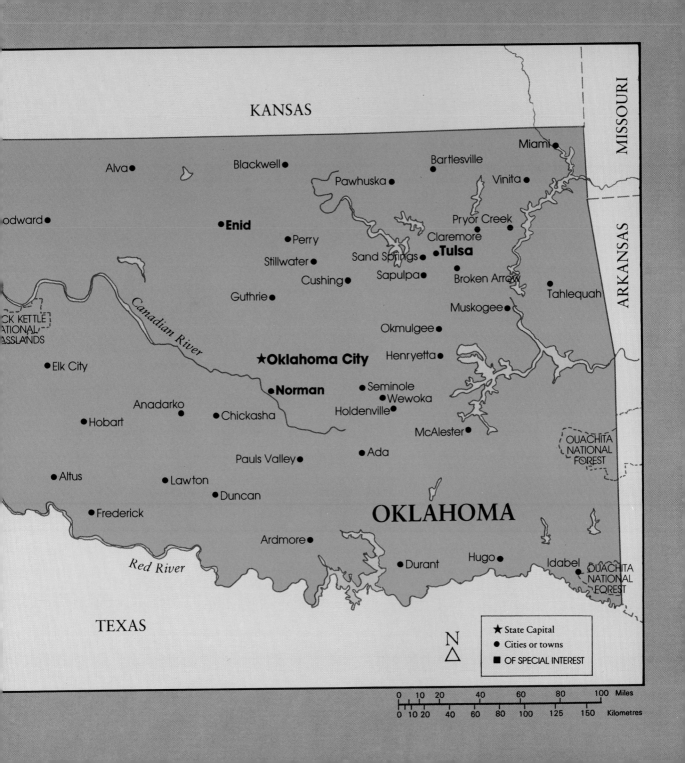

The Ouachita National Forest is part of the Ouachita Mountain Range, in southeastern Oklahoma. This heavily wooded region supplies the state's lumber industry.

The Land

Oklahoma is bounded on the west by New Mexico and Texas, on the north by Colorado and Kansas, on the east by Missouri and Arkansas, and on the south by Texas. The state has 10 main land regions. They are the Ozark Plateau, the Prairie Plains, the Ouachita Mountains, the Sandstone Hills, the Arbuckle Mountains, the Wichita Mountains, the Red River Region, the Red Beds Plains, the Gypsum Hills, and the High Plains.

The Ozark Plateau is located in northeastern Oklahoma and extends into Missouri and Arkansas. It is a hilly region with many streams and river valleys. Beef cattle, oats, corn, and soybeans are raised here.

The Prairie Plains are west and south of the Ozark Plateau. This is an important cattle-ranching area, and also a region of vegetable crops. Most of the state's coal and much of its oil are found in this region.

The Ouachita Mountains are located in southeastern Oklahoma on the Arkansas border. These sandstone ridges divided by narrow valleys are the roughest land surface in the state. The most important industry here is lumbering.

The Sandstone Hills extend from the Kansas border south to the Red River. This is a region of low hills, partially covered with forests

Much of eastern Oklahoma is characterized by plateaus and low mountains.

of blackjack and post oak. The region has important petroleum reserves and contains dairy, hog, and fruit farms.

The Arbuckle Mountains form a small wedge in south-central Oklahoma. These hills were once mighty mountains, now worn down by erosion to form a rocky landscape that is largely unsuitable for agriculture.

The granite peaks of the Wichita Mountains rise over a small section of southwestern Oklahoma. Little farming is done here; most of the area lies within the Fort Sill military reservation and a federal wildlife refuge watered by numerous streams.

The Red River Region consists of gently rolling prairies and wooded land in southeastern Oklahoma, on the Texas border. Cotton, peanuts, corn, and vegetables are grown in the sandy soil of this fertile area.

The Red Beds Plains, named for the soft red sandstone and shale beneath them, form a strip down the central part of Oklahoma from Kansas to Texas. Livestock, cotton, and wheat are raised here.

The Gypsum Hills are located west of the Red Bed Plains and rise to 200 feet above sea level. Some sheep, cattle, and wheat are raised here.

The High Plains comprise an area of level grassland in the northwest, including the Panhandle region. The land rises from about 2,000 feet in the eastern section to 4,978 feet at Black Mesa, the highest point in the state. This westernmost section of Oklahoma supports sorghum, broomcorn, wheat, and cattle.

The main river systems in Oklahoma are the Red and the Arkansas. The state has about 100 small natural lakes and more than 200 man-made lakes.

The weather in Oklahoma is primarily warm and dry—typical of the south-central states. July temperatures climb to 90 degrees Fahrenheit and above, with an average of 83 degrees F. In January the average temperature is around 40 degrees F. The state receives up to 25 inches of snow per year in the northern Panhandle, with as little as 2 inches falling in the southeast. Rainfall is heaviest in southeastern Oklahoma.

The Quartz Mountains belong to the Wichita chain, in southwestern Oklahoma, where underlying granite makes much of the land unsuitable for farming.

A Comanche treks across Oklahoma's snowy plains on horseback. The Comanche were among the many Indian tribes who originally inhabited the region.

The History

This "ghost dance shirt," made by Pawnee Indians native to Oklahoma, was worn by elders of the tribe during sacred ceremonies.

The first inhabitants of what is now Oklahoma were Plains Indians, whose migratory way of life was dependent upon the great buffalo herds that roamed the Western prairies. Tribes encountered by European explorers included the Arapaho, Caddo, Cheyenne, Comanche, Kiowa, Osage, Pawnee, and Wichita.

The first Europeans to enter the Oklahoma area were Francisco Vásquez de Coronado and his men, who arrived in 1541. Another band of Spanish explorers, led by Hernando de Soto, also came into the region in search of the legendary Seven Cities of Cibola. The Spanish failed to find the gold they sought, and left the Indians undisturbed until the late 17th century. Then French fur traders and explorers passed through in the wake of the French explorer Robert Cavelier, known as La Salle, who had claimed all the land drained by the Mississippi River for his country in 1682.

What is now Oklahoma became United States territory with the Louisiana Purchase of 1803. Subdivisions of the vast Louisiana Territory resulted in Oklahoma's becoming part of the Missouri

Territory and then of the Arkansas Territory. The region's first large-scale settlements were made in the 1820s by Choctaw and Chickasaw Indians. In the 1830s they were pushed by federal authorities to leave their traditional homes and move farther west so that white settlers could move into them. The Indians established permanent villages, farmed, set up schools and law courts of their own, and created a written version of their language. In 1859 they joined with the Cherokee, Creek, and Seminole to form a federation known as the Five Civilized Tribes because they had adopted many

Fur trader and pioneer Pierre Chouteau led an Osage Indian band into present-day Oklahoma and established the first trading post near Salina in 1802.

Millions of Texas cattle were driven along the Chisholm Trail, between the Rio Grande and Abilene, Kansas, during the 1860s. The trail passed through central Oklahoma, and "cow towns" and cities flourished along the route.

customs of the European and American settlers. The Oklahoma area was designated Indian Territory, with a portion assigned to each of these five tribes, which were to be self-governing tribal nations within their assigned territories.

Between 1830 and 1846, 20,000 Creeks from Georgia and Alabama, 5,000 Choctaws from Mississippi and Louisiana, 4,000 Chickasaws from Mississippi, and 3,000 Seminoles from Florida were forced into this area. In 1838 and 1839, some 16,000 Cherokees were marched west from their lands in North Carolina, Tennessee, and Georgia by troops under the command of General Winfield Scott. About one-fourth of those forced west over this "Trail of Tears" died en route of hunger, disease, cold, and exhaustion.

After the Civil War of 1861–1865, homesteaders were pushing westward in ever greater numbers. For a time the government refused to move the Indians and punished white trespassers, but eventually the treaty that had promised the Indians their lands for "as long as grass shall grow and rivers run" was broken. Nearby areas were filling up with settlers eager to encroach upon the Indian reservations. During the 1870s and 1880s, homesteaders called "Boomers" urged the government to open Indian Territory to white settlement. The government yielded and bought more than 3,000,000 acres from the Creek and Seminole tribes. Some 1,900,000 acres in central Oklahoma were declared open for settlement as of high noon of April 22, 1889. Thousands of homesteaders waited on the border until a pistol was fired to signify that the territory was open for settlement, then stampeded into the area to choose the best sites for towns and farms. (Those who entered the region before the land rush officially began were called "Sooners"—hence the state's nickname.) Some 50,000 people moved into Oklahoma on the first day. Subsequent "runs" and lotteries brought additional thousands, especially after the Cherokee Outlet was opened to white settlement in 1893.

Twin Territories were created in 1890, when maps showed two separate entities: Indian Territory and Oklahoma Territory. As

additional settlers arrived, federal commissioners began to prepare the population for statehood. The Indian nations were dissolved, and what remained of the treaty lands were allotted to individual Indians rather than to their tribes. Indian efforts to create a separate state called Sequoyah were defeated, and the combined Twin Territories became the 46th state in 1907.

During the territorial period, farming had developed rapidly and oil had been discovered. Expansion continued until the 1920s, when drought and a drop in farm prices brought economic problems, worsened by the Great Depression of the 1930s. Thousands of farmers left their land to become migrant "Okies," as they were called, when prolonged heat and high winds created the Dust Bowl.

During World War II, Oklahoma's crops, fuel, and livestock were needed for the war effort, and growth resumed. Exploration for petroleum and natural gas brought new discoveries. Today, improved irrigation and water power have benefited both farming and industry.

The first Oklahoma schools were founded by missionaries to educate Indian children in the 1820s. The territorial legislature provided for public education for white children in 1890. By 1907, 10 colleges and universities were operating in the newly created state.

A view of Oklahoma City in 1890, the year in which Congress passed an act establishing the Oklahoma Territory in the western part of the state. Eastern Oklahoma had been designated Indian Territory in 1825.

The People

More than 67 percent of the people in Oklahoma live in Oklahoma City, Tulsa, and other cities and towns. More than 95 percent of them were born in the United States; almost 6 percent of them are American Indians. The largest religious groups in the state are the Baptists, Episcopalians, Methodists, and Presbyterians.

In the field of the arts, outstanding Oklahomans include the classical composer Roy Harris (Lincoln County) and the prima ballerina Maria Tallchief (Fairfax). The great humorist Will Rogers,

Attorney and diplomat Patrick J. Hurley was born to a Choctaw family in Indian Territory in 1883. He represented the Choctaw Nation in Washington, D.C., served as secretary of war under President Herbert Hoover, and represented President Franklin D. Roosevelt in dealings with the Allies during World War II.

Oklahoma City, the state's capital, is also its largest city, with a population of more than 400,000.

Humorist, cowboy, actor, and news commentator Will Rogers was born in 1879 in Oologah, Indian Territory, to a family of mixed Irish and Cherokee ancestry. He is remembered as a warm, down-to-earth observer of the American scene.

of mixed Irish-American and Cherokee parentage, was born in Oologah, then known as Indian Territory. A renowned athlete who excelled in track, football, and baseball—Jim Thorpe—was born in Prague. Oklahomans in the entertainment field include singer Anita Bryant, television's "Odd Couple" actor Tony Randall, and film director Blake Edwards, who directed many of the popular "Pink Panther" films and others including *Victor/Victoria* and *10*.

Indian City, U.S.A.

Will Rogers Memorial.

OF SPECIAL INTEREST

IN OKLAHOMA CITY: *Cowboy Hall of Fame and Western Heritage Center*
This complex houses a major art collection depicting America's Western heritage.

NEAR ANADARKO: *Indian City, U.S.A.*
Oklahoma's original people are commemorated by replicas of Plains Indian
settlements of the early 1800s.

IN CLAREMORE: *Will Rogers Memorial*
A stone ranch house displays exhibits about the much-loved cowboy humorist and
memorabilia of Indian and pioneer days.

NEAR LAWTON: *Fort Sill*
Established in 1869, Fort Sill has three national historic sites: Stone Corral, Old
Guardhouse, and an artillery museum.

IN MUSKOGEE: *Five Civilized Tribes Museum*
The museum contains exhibits on the history and culture of the five Southeastern
tribes who were forcibly relocated to Oklahoma in the early nineteenth
century.

For more information write:
THE TOURISM MARKETING SERVICES
DIVISION OF TOURISM AND RECREATION
505 WILL ROGERS MEMORIAL BUILDING
OKLAHOMA CITY, OKLAHOMA 73105

FURTHER READING

Bailey, Bernadine. *Picture Book of Oklahoma*, rev. ed. Whitman, 1967.
Carpenter, Allan. *Oklahoma*, rev. ed. Childrens Press, 1979.
Fradin, Dennis B. *Oklahoma in Words and Pictures*. Childrens Press, 1981.
Gibson, Arrell M. *The Oklahoma Story*. University of Oklahoma Press, 1978.
Goble, Danney. *Progressive Oklahoma: The Making of a New Kind of State.*
University of Oklahoma Press, 1979.
Morgan, H. Wayne, and Hodges, Anne. *Oklahoma: A Bicentennial History.*
Norton, 1977.

INDEX

Numbers in italics refer to illustrations

Photo Credits/Acknowledgments

Photos on pages 5, 6–7 (Robyn Horn), 9, 10 (Robyn Horn), 11, 12, 15 (Pat Pickett), 16 (A.C Haralson), courtesy of the Arkansas Department of Parks and Tourism; pages 17, 18–19, 20, 22, 23, 26, courtesy of The Kansas Department of Economic Development; pages 27, 28–29, 30–31, 32, 35 (top), 36, courtesy of The Louisiana Office of Tourism; pages 37, 38–39, 41, 42, 44, 45, 48, courtesy of The Missouri Division of Tourism; pages 49, 50–51, 52, 54, 55, 60, 62, courtesy of The Oklahoma Division of Tourism/Fred W. Marvel; pages 25, 46, 47, National Portrait Gallery; page 56, Museum, of the American Indian; pages 34 (top), 59, Ne York Public Library/Stokes Collection.

Cover photograph courtesy of the Arkansas Department of Parks and Tourism.

The Publisher would like to thank Cathy Bradshaw of the Arkansas Department of Parks and tourism, Mary McCaffrey of the Kansas Department of Economic Development, Al Godoy of the Louisiana Office of Tourism, Steve Kappler of the Missouri Division of Tourism, and Fre W. Marvel, of the Oklahoma Division of Tourism for their gracious assistance in the preparation of this book.